LIFE IS A SPECIAL EVENT:
Organize, Plan, and Celebrate Your Life

To Laura,

All our Love
All our Life
We are the Glory!

Light + Love
Victory.

Carol

LIFE IS A SPECIAL EVENT:
Organize, Plan, and Celebrate Your Life

Carol Moxam

2016

Copyright © 2016 by Carol Moxam Inc.

All rights reserved. This book or any portion thereof may not be reproduced or used in any manner whatsoever without the express written permission of the publisher except for the use of brief quotations in a book review or scholarly journal.

First Printing: 2016

ISBN 978-1-775-00010-5

Carol Moxam Inc.
www.carolmoxam.com

Cover designed by Javraj Sagoo
Sketch designed by Karina Goel
Interior designed by Alexander Ambroz

Ordering Information:

Special discounts are available on quantity purchases by corporations, associations, educators, and others. For details, contact the publisher at the above listed address.

U.S. trade bookstores and wholesalers: Please contact Moxam Publishing Inc. Tel: +1 (888) 384-5142; or email moxamc@gmail.com

Dedication

To my loving parents.
To my extraordinary sons, Jake and Hunter.
To my best of friend Jenny.
To the event professionals in the world.
You are all my sources for celebration!

Life is a Special Event

Your life is a gifted period of existence here on earth. You are a soul living a human experience.

You are creating your life by designing a series of unique moments celebrating your best self while satisfying your specific needs in fulfilling a life with purpose.

Experience life.

Contents

Acknowledgements xiii

Preface xvii

Introduction 1

Chapter 1: Create Your Special Event Life 3

Chapter 2: Strategic Planning of You 6

Chapter 3: Your Life Purpose 17

Chapter 4: Design Your Life 23

Chapter 5: Life's Budget – It's Your Time 26

Chapter 6: The Venue – It is You 32

Chapter 7: Life's Delicious Menu 37

Chapter 8: Your Life Entertainment 41

Chapter 9: A Live Production 43

Chapter 10: Scripting the Plan 50

Chapter 11: Life's Invitations 53

Chapter 12: Capture Life 61

Conclusion 63

About The Author 65

Acknowledgements

This book itself is an acknowledgement of the pivotal people in the special event of my life. Firstly I want to thank my Mom and Dad, for love and support. My two extraordinary sons, Jake and Hunter, who are special.

My thanks to my sister Gillian, for generous contribution of listening. Gillian creates loving events with her husband Sham, and for my nieces and nephews, Amanda, Justin, Ben and Nicole. And to my magical and loving brother, Ken, who never misses a family special event.

Thank you to my miraculous best friend, Jenny, a master of living compassion, ridiculous fun, simplicity, and life adventures, for the contribution in creating a paradigm shift in my health and life balance. And to Mateo and Jenna, the next generation of special events to the world.

I want to extend my thanks to all my team leadership program participants for your contribution in being powerful communication. And to the young people who have evolved into event leaders through my mentorship program.

A special mention to Carrie and Daniel for your contribution to bridging my career path from event management to lifestyle and leadership coaching. You both inspire what is possible in family and business.

Thanks to my magical friend Dawn and her princess Sophia. Proof that Disney dreams do come true and that in a one momentous meeting you can create a friendship that lasts a lifetime.

My heartfelt appreciation goes to one of my first teachers in the realm of special event planning, Suzanne, who demonstrated exceptional leadership in the industry by empowering generations of planners through professional certifications. She left a legacy of leadership and commitment to the event industry.

To event professionals worldwide: you are the source for celebration. Please remember that your health and your relationship with yourself is the finest event you will ever produce.

To Frederick, for your contribution in demonstrating how this living life as a special event every day by creating Frederick's Life Party.

Marta, my trainer, thank you for contributing to my working venue of health in strengthening my foundation.

Thank you Cindy, my messenger, and the source of my connection to my family roots. We invent and defy expectations of "self."

And finally, a moment of gratitude for YOU. Thank you for taking the time to invest in you. This moment is to honour you. Now, let's get this party started.

Preface

There is one specific event unique to you: your birthday. A birth date represents a new cycle of life events that completes a circuit every 365 days. This is your day to celebrate your time on this earth and bathe in your own brilliance.

The journey I am committed to taking you on will provide an opportunity for you to design a theme for your life and to invent your best self as "The Real Party". This is not an ordinary event, this is a "Special Event", and you will want to work with the very best teams and resources to make it all happen.

Many of us grow up living a linear and inherited life that is sometimes a safe life. We follow the path of our previous generations for school, work, marriage, and retirement. Once we are out of school, rarely does anyone ever stop to tell us how to design our own future.

When working in special events, as professional planners we create new futures with events. This is our business; we do this for our clients. The client calls us with an event concept and requests we build a proposed plan, and with acceptance we then execute it. We get to dream up and create magical events. It all begins with an idea, an inspiration of what is possible.

Are you ready to take this on in your life? It is your turn to design your life as a special event. Dream big and create your vision.

Start with brainstorming ideas for a future event, evolve them in your thoughts, draft a story board and spend the next three, six or twelve months planning, coordinating, and finally producing your most spectacular event life.

When you execute a well thought out plan with focus and manage the moments with your self-guided leadership you may begin to notice your life expanding with miracles.

There are moments in life when you feel you are important and want to do your own things. There is nothing wrong in feeling this way. When we listen to our self and reach for our higher self and what is good for us, we encounter our own strength. It gives us the essential power to do what is good for us regardless of what anyone else may say or think.

When you feel confident, you move forward without the need to convince anyone as to why you are doing what you do.

Every event has key elements. You are most likely familiar with these basic ones: catering, decor, venue, entertainment and guests. It is important that you recognize that this book is not about the events you attend, it is about you, and you are the real live event!

You are both the foundation and the location for every event that will take place. Begin by looking at your elements and then applying management skills that professional planners use to co-ordinate. Your scheduled project plan includes your budget, which advises how to invest your time each day.

You bring a unique gift to this world. That gift is so supreme, so beautiful, so all-encompassing that this is your reminder to elevate it into prominence and to create a new consciousness of yourself in life. This gift is to be seen whether you are an engineer, a singer, a designer, a veterinarian, a football player, an accountant, a teacher, a police officer, or even a doctor. When you look at who you are in your career can you see how these events have shaped your life?

Have a look into the mirror. Who are you, what do you see? What do you say to yourself? Are you taking the highest care of yourself? If the answer is yes, then great, you are already on the path of living a designed life. You may be at the stage of inventing what is next for you. If the answer is no, and you are thinking you are not ok, often unconsciously, then this costs you a lot of energy. Remember you are perfect and you now have the privilege to explore and discover yourself newly inside of this book. Make a choice and be aware of your choices.

Life fulfillment comes from the magical moments experienced in joy, happiness, and victories. In addition, many moments in life are challenging. These landmark events expand your growth and power in life for all that you need and require in each moment.

It was not until much later on in my career, when I worked with my life coaches, that I realized I was a master at producing spectacular events for clients and that this was not reflected in planning time for myself. Countless hours were invested in working on my business and not my life. This is where the imbalance of how I spent my time was one-sided with work and not on my pleasure side, which focuses on taking care of me. Now that I am aware that my life is my business it certainly has me investing in all areas of myself, not just my work.

In professionally planned events there is the anticipation that experiences during the event might not go as planned. Be prepared to work with a team to resolve any issues calmly and efficiently. These very same skills you can use in your life for not being worried or afraid of what might happen. Focus is on what is happening right now. You are creating moment by moment a solution about how choose to be in the face challenges. This takes practice, and it is the mastery you develop in yourself to become present.

There is no time for replays in special events; every moment in an event is live. The same philosophy applies in your life.

Ultimately, every event in your life is your free will to choose the outcome. In other words, you say exactly how it will go. Every challenge does fade away old ideas and it simultaneously creates new possibilities. Surprises make it fascinating when you see them.

As part of this book, it is my intention to give you tools to acknowledge, accept, and to manage powerfully how to move through these life events. The beauty of these new experiences is that you will be challenged in every aspect.

Your life requires a structure for being organized, having a plan, communicating with yourself honestly and heading in a desired direction at all times. Where you focus your attention you will produce results. Today something might happen that changes it all. Notice how you can discover a new truth each day.

A plan is a comprehensive document to crystallize strategies related to your life goals and objectives. If you have a solid life plan in place that is managed objectively any disagreements and unplanned events can be resolved. Review your goals every day and use them to motivate you for what is next at your life's special events.

Carol Moxam

Introduction

I began writing this book because I saw a need for event planners, specifically, to recognize that their own life is a special event. Event planning is one of the most stressful jobs in the world. And while planners are multi-talented and can handle the stress and challenges of their jobs very well. They often do not give their own lives the attention they deserve.

Who am I and what do I know about planning events and planning your life? I have spent over 20 years as a professional in special events planning. I have coordinated many grand occasions with the finest of details including extravagant entertainment, spectacular decor, and delightfully tasteful chef prepared meals. These events connected people to heartfelt moments, created joy, and saw their guests freely expressing themselves within the environment I created.

In my personal life I have experienced events of happiness and joy and events of challenge and emotion. The events that shaped my life the most are the difficult ones. Many have been challenging—especially those involving my health, finances, and relationships—but without them I may never have written this book. They have served as golden lessons for me. I share to help others to understand the importance of their own life events and how your life experiences are shaped by our own view of life.

You see, each year of our lives is marked by moments and events, some big, some small, some earth-moving, some adventurous and some exciting. What was common in all these events, the experiences.

My journey began with me examining my own experiences and realizing that while I was really good at my event profession and not so great at planning my personal life events. I saw the opportunity to apply event management skills in my life. I tweaked these strategies and ultimately came up with an entirely new lifestyle.

Use this book to inspire you in choosing your dream lifestyle. Have a life where you get to create and have extravagant fun. This is your VIP invitation to yourself to plan your life as a special event—to approach every day as though you were walking the red carpet. What you want is to experience life fully. It's remarkably simple.

Carol Moxam

Chapter I: Create Your Special Event Life

Your life is a special event. It is live and happening right now. It is a one-time event because there is only ever going to be one of you on this planet in this lifetime.

You are living this grand celebration and experience called being human. From the very day you were born, your life was destined with a purpose to fulfill on.

When you stop and think about it, your life is a series of important moments happening day after day, week after week, month after month, and year after year. Each of those moments form the incredibly special event that is your life.

Those moments make series' of events both planned and unplanned that lead up to the main event: a life filled with purpose. This book is about making sure that you are the source of creation, organization, planning and celebrating your life.

How can you take your life to the level of grandeur that brings out your best self every day? What if you were the professional event manager of your life? What would it look like if you started to define your life as a special event? What design would you choose to excite you?

You can design your own spectacular and themed lifestyle by learning and applying the skills and processes used in professional event management. We do this in special events planning is about bringing dreams to life using our own creativity. So why not apply those same principles to planning your life?

The special events industry is all about fun, excitement, happiness, creativity, and rising to the challenge. Event professionals around the world create unbelievable and incredible events that connect, inspire, and celebrate. The role of the planner is to work in the background to meet crazy deadlines, manage impossible budgets, and achieve breathtaking results. Does this sound familiar?

When you reflect upon the most remarkable, outstanding, and satisfying moments in your life, the ones where you opened your heart, laughed or struggled, you can often pinpoint when you have most fully participated in the privilege of being alive. These moments comprise life's most special events. But did you know you can also design a life for yourself that cultivates an environment where you will experience more of those moments.

It starts with determining your life's purpose and then take an in-depth look at all the elements that make up your life today.

Just as with any event planning, this involves looking at things like strategizing, defining the events purpose, design, budgeting, venue, catering, entertainment, production, invitations and documentation. By carefully examining all these different elements you will create a vision for your life that you want to achieve, and a plan to make it all happen.

Along the way you will encounter challenges but you can learn how to overcome them with self-management, calmness and clarity. Event professionals are well trained at this to deal with the many unplanned moments that come with every event.

Personal emotions often get in the way of making powerful choices when it comes to your own life events. The key to learning here is for you to work with facts not the story's that get made up in what is happening. Once you have all the facts, go ahead and make an intelligent decision to keep your events moving forward and onto what's next in your plans.

There is no need to wait for a big occasion to start your planning now is the time to actualize your most precious and desired dreams.

Chapter 2: Strategic Planning of You

What every successful event has in common is the foundation of a strong strategic plan. There are five phases to creating such a plan: research, design, planning, coordination, and evaluation.

As the event manager for your life, it is time to create a strategic plan for yourself. You are likely already a planner in some areas of your life. In fact, somehow I suspect that you take care of everyone and everything else in your life first and that you rarely get around to meeting your own needs. You find yourself behind the scenes making it all work seamlessly for everyone else. But now it is your turn to be the center of attention.

Research

The purpose of your research is to pinpoint the needs, desires, and expectations most important to living the life you want. Include in your examination of yourself what you want in your health, relationships, and work. These are on-going events that make up the bulk of your life.

I completed a useful exercise with my naturopath where she asked me to write down all the happiest moments as well as those events that were not so satisfying that affected my life the most.

When you review the experiences of your life in great detail you may start to notice similar events that have taken place throughout your life.

This is just the beginning of understanding yourself and to building a new strategy. Collect and communicate your findings and write the details in a notebook. Seeing your life's events written down on paper helps you to better understand their impact on your life.

Thoughtfully and confidently, now reveal to yourself what is important to you, and what you discovered that will support you in achieving your life goals. Reflect on how all your past events have shaped your life to date. You can use this research to build on the expectations of what you intend to accomplish next in your life. Next step is designing your life. Begin with the end in mind.

Design

Now that you have listed expectations for yourself and what you want in the research phase you are ready to create a general design blueprint for your ideas on what you intend to accomplish and in which areas of your life you will focus on.

A blueprint lays out in detail a desired outcome of your special event. Spend as much time as you need doing this because you will want to be able to refer to it frequently.

Look at your life and ask yourself: "Did I design my life or is someone else managing it for me?" The answer to this question might have you look at life today and imagine how you are going to create your events of tomorrow using what you learn in this book.

Here is a glimpse of what your life may look like without having a design. Every day you wake up, go to work, come home, go to bed, and repeat. Often you are so rooted in our current processes that you unconsciously allow them to define who you are and what you are going to accomplish at a particular phase or stage of our life. When you design a blueprint for your life you can align your actions to produce the outcome you really want. The blueprint becomes your tool for living a life by your choice.

The purpose of the design phase is to turn your dreams into workable plans with thoughtful design.

There are numerous ways to begin this process. The source of your design inspiration will come from your research. To keep things simple I recommend using a timeline of 90 days for planning a specific element of your life. This allows you to build a foundation for which you can expand on in the future. By using a shorter period of time and focusing on one particular area in your life you have time to learn, practice, and refine your event planning skills.

Write down as many ideas you can on areas of your life you want to design. This can be a list of the various components of your life event elements. Elements might include your health, your important relationships, entertainment and activities in your life, and budget. Next from this list pick one area of your life that you want to go to work on in building a design in this time period.

Provide specific details on the overview of your design element and include the date by when your event will happen, the time of your event, and the location.

Next, choose a theme related to what you want that is fun. A theme is a unifying idea that connects with who you are and gives focus and inspiration. A theme might be related to your favourite movie, hobbies, theatre performances, sports, art, literature, dance, or any other activity.

A theme gives you something new to say about your day-to-day events in your life. Remember, your life's special events will be a reflection of your imagination. Keep in mind that the theme can set the tone for your life events. Rotate these themes regularly to maintain an element of surprise.

A theme is a meaningful interpretation of your event's goals and objectives. It functions as the elevator pitch for your life and helps people understand in a very short period of time what you intend to accomplish. You do not need a theme for your life to be successful but why pass up a way to encapsulate your mission to the people and experiences in your life. It is a unique experience and is what made a tremendous difference in my life when I did this.

I theme every quarter of my life. A theme I once used over a 90-day period was "Travel Wellness Adventures." I knew I was planning my holiday to Greece and created my life events to experience both relaxation and adventure. What showed up in my life planning was as a big surprise. I went away on four different trips during that same period. Be prepared to expect the unexpected as you build a blueprint. You can make a plan, you plan the plan, and then get ready for all the unplanned events.

Imagination is your fuel for design; be as creative as your mind will allow. Imagine your life as you want it to be with your chosen element and describe in detail what you see. How do you look in the future? At this point do not impose any budget or limitations on yourself. The sky is the limit for your ideas; write them all down.

It is important to give yourself time to refine your own design techniques. Write as precisely and descriptively as possible. Declare what you intend to accomplish and the steps towards achieving that objective.

To focus your creativity begin with a broad statement of what you want to achieve over a specific period of time in your life. If, for any reason, you cannot see what your purpose is look at your research and ask yourself "what were the moments in my life that gave me the most happiness and joy?"

You are creating a personal vision for what matters to you. Learn to embrace the blessings that are available to you during every moment of your life in creating those moments.

Planning

The planning period is typically the most involved period of the event management process. Without a plan you may notice how disorganization is obvious and when there are frequent changes in plans. But the better job you have done in the research and design phases the shorter the planning period will be.

The planning phase is about timing—setting out the length of time you have available to complete an event. I have suggested using a 90-day time period for planning your life events.

Pay attention to how much time you spend on planning. Do you rush your plans and skip over key details? Or perhaps you spend many hours in this phase? Or for some you may notice you do not have planning currently in your daily life. Regardless of what planning methods you have done in the past you can use this strategy to plan your life now.

This phase is you get into the practical dimensions of what it is going to take to fulfill your goal; you will be working your plan backwards step-by-step. Do not forget to factor in contingency time for unplanned events. Leave time in your schedule open. Too many of us fill up our calendars with back to back events and there is little or no time for unexpected events to happen.

Your plans should be a constant reference source with the theme that inspires your day-to-day activities. Determine your daily activities based on achieving your desired outcomes.

Be prepared for challenges. Real learning takes place outside your comfort zone when you put yourself on the line and take chances. Unless you do this you never achieve the extraordinary results that make your life a truly special event. Over time this adventurous state of mind will become your new standard, replacing fear, complacency, self-doubt, and resistance with a sense of adventure, excitement, and wonderment.

When you begin to examine your planning in relation to your designed blueprint you can build a comprehensive and customized checklist of what your criteria for your best self might look like.

Once you have finalized your blueprint and planning create a story board to help visualize your life as a special event. A story board includes colours, your theme, visuals of your outcomes, drawing sketches or pictures of what your event might look like, and be sure to include a detailed description describing your future event.

Coordinating

Coordination is the mastery where you execute your design and plans in real time. You manage your time, your actions, and even the smallest minute segments. There are hundreds of details to coordinating daily in your life. You want to be able to establish and adjust its tempo and keep it focused on your blueprint. You must be able to balance every component in your life.

During your coordinating phase, you can take a long hard look at each of your life event elements and identify any gaps in planning that might hinder the progression of your plan. It is useful to continually review your progress weekly.

What makes a competent event planner is the ability to make good decisions at a moment's notice.

Evaluating

Being able to evaluate yourself is one of the most important factors for success. Event professionals continuously evaluate. How you do this by asking yourself questions like: "How could I do this better?" Self-evaluation helps you to learn and improve anything. Document your lessons and use this for future events.

After you become comfortable evaluating yourself it can also be helpful to ask others what they think you could do to improve. Try it first with people you know well. When you gain confidence asking people you are comfortable with you can then start asking others for their thoughts. These people may be much better at it then you are, at the same level, or not nearly as good. If you are willing to ask and listen to them sincerely, you will reach your potential much quicker than you would on your own. It is difficult to do and requires a fair amount of self-confidence on your part but the results will be well worth it in the end.

Practice is critical to everything you are doing to create your strategic plan. This is because the mind understands but it is the body that learns. Understanding can occur in an instant but real learning takes time. Be generous in evaluating your own performance in events and be patient with yourself as you learn what does and does not work for you in this process.

You are the Special Event

Using the five phases for strategic planning will help you to envision you future with certainty and clarity. Determine what actions you want to take to produce the desired outcomes you designed and make it happen. You are the producer in charge of it all and you can create it any way you choose at any moment.

Although you may begin the event process during any phase it is important that all phases be visited regularly, updated, reviewed, and understood.

When things get chaotic, your strategic plan acts as a map to remind you where you want to be and how you can get back on the path to your destination.

Chapter 3: Your Life Purpose

What is this all about? What exactly are you creating with your life? Every moment each man or woman creates his own future.

An event brings people together for a particular purpose. "Special" means unusually good or extraordinary - something not to be missed. Your life as special event, then, is an extraordinary happening bringing you together with your best self and enjoying experiences with your best guests. It is an event with a distinct purpose. This is all about you.

What you may be asking yourself at this moment is, "Am I preparing, planning, and producing my life events? Do I know where I am going from here?" If you do not know what your plans are I can promise you someone else is about to handle your life planning for you.

The good news is that going forward you are now the event manager for all your life events. When you are at the source of creating, designing and planning your life events, you can use this practice to keep taking your life experiences to the next level. There are no limits to what you can accomplish.

What is your life purpose? Your past events may tell a story of your happiest moments, and your saddest ones. However, your past does not define who you are today. You have choice and t free will to define who you are and what you want to do.

When you are inspired with great purpose you can be used by it. You may notice everything begins to work for you. Fulfillment and inspiration on this creativity will have you live your life as the real party, as the real deal.

Creativity is all about producing something new. The specialness and success of your event depends in large measure on the creativity you are able to bring to it.

The time of year when most of us get clear about our purpose is New Year`s Day. Why is this? Perhaps it is because we have a blank slate. It is a great time to reflect and the perfect time to create. Why not take on each new day of your life the same?

Can you imagine how your focus will shift when you plan every quarter of your life versus just once a year? You start with a blank slate. You create who you are, you say what your purpose is, and you define your life experiences. You will be surprised at how much this can impact your life.

The two greatest days of your life are the day you were born, and the day you find out what your purpose is, but if you do not know what your purpose is then you do not know why you are here and it can be hard to keep going.

Being born on the first day of the year for me is special. I was born on New Year's Day in Scotland. On New Year's at midnight all around the world there is celebrations bringing in the New Year. I want everyone to celebrate every day and with the same excitement and reflection. Celebrating the moments that matter most to us and being with our best guests.

The magic for your event begins with intention and intelligent execution. When you become intent, it sets up a path for attainment. Intention is a strong purpose or aim accompanied by a determination to produce a desired result. When you have a strong will it will not permit anything to interfere with your inner desire.

As you design your life, your feelings of self-importance are what makes you feel special. Let's take a look at the concept of being special. It is essential you have a strong self-concept and that you feel unique.

Your natural state in special events is joy. It is only natural for you to experience this feeling when you are in harmony at your own party. Monitor your event regularly by checking in on yourself. Are you feeling good at your event? If at any time the answer is no, then ask yourself if you are at the right party.

You can customize your event to remain differentiated. There is only one of you in this lifetime special event. How will you serve in your life?

There is nothing more fulfilling than making the lives of others a little better. When you live a life on purpose contributing to others you will see how your life purpose gets fulfilled.

By defining the level of influence you want to have in your life, you can have clear goals and objectives to support the plan. When you analyze your self-purpose it will answer the "Why must you have this event." This is a declaration applied to every decision you make aligned with your why.

To produce consistently effective events, we begin by defining your event overview with the five 'W's of public relations, including who, what, when, where, and why. Looking back at your life will provide a good resource of research for you to build upon.

"Why" is the first question to ask yourself. Why are you living this life experience? What is my "why" in the world? This is very personal and derived from your inner most desires.

The second step is to ask "Who" will my life serve in this lifetime. Go beyond who you know yourself today. The level of commitment to your actions will help you define who this event is being produced for. Examining your career, relationships, and health may give insight into the answers on this step.

The third step is to determine "When" this event will be held. Naturally this is your event is your whole life. However for the purpose of planning I suggest using the 90-day timeline allowing time to prepare and execute your specific desired outcomes. Shorter periods of planning gives you the satisfaction in seeing your events unfold each quarter and to celebrate successes. If you are one of the adventurous ones, go ahead and plan your entire year's events including the quarterly planning. Use your strategy to revamp any planning you may have missed in the initial stages.

The fourth step involves determining "Where" your event will be held. The decision on where will affect many areas of your life and the decisions you make each quarter. If your event takes place in your current location then use this as your "where". For others who enjoy traveling, take on discovering yourself newly in that destination.

The fifth and final "W" is "What" is the event you are developing and producing? Your "what" is the product of your research in strategizing your needs, wants, and desires that satisfy your internal and external requirements of you - your best self.

Once you have the five questions thoroughly answered, it is necessary to turn your deliberation to "how" to allocate the resources to produce the maximum benefit for your life. Resources are the people who will contribute their talents to your life event.

Always know that your heart is your best tool for discovering your true purpose and passion. By doing what you love you will be continually inspired. There are no limitations on what you can accomplish in your life. When you look in your heart to find your desires, you are living a purposeful life.

Chapter 4: Design Your Life

In a nutshell, designing your life as a special event is about shaping your environment and molding your lifestyle. It is your life, your plan, and you call all the shots. Ultimately how you implement a design-led approach to your life it can help you to transform your dreams into workable plans.

The tone of your design is created in your blueprint. Through your thoughts, written, and spoken words. You create your events. They can be shared as series of stories.

When an event decor architect designs an event his vision is articulated with mathematical precision. He can visualize it so clearly that he can go out to the venue with his clients and walk them through the plans in intricate detail. Without that kind of detailed plan, the foundation will not stand. Your vision needs to be articulated with that same commitment to detail in mind.

The ability to see your potential future in your mind's eye in glorious technicolor is yet another step towards achieving your goals.

Your life design exists in your language. What you say, you create. When you say your events will happen - they will happen. Remember this as you encounter the many distractions that try to take you away from your main events.

Share your events with others. Tell them what you are up to. It is exciting and if your purpose has your heart beating every time you speak it you will know you are on the right path. You are the architect designer rendering your vision with the finest detail.

Designers make it their mission to answer questions fully to design the environment of event experiences that are aligned with the overall purpose of an event. Step into the future, see it, feel it, imagine the experience of what you are creating. Describe in detail what you intend to happen in each area of your life.

One tool that event designers use to help with visualization is a vision board. It provides you with a tangible expression of your vision that allows you to see the steps needed to reach your desired outcomes, and uses images of those outcomes to inspire your all of your senses.

You will find that putting your vision where you see it daily helps you focus. Place it and reference it often to remind you of your plan and the actions you are going take to fulfill this plan.

Your personal decor is your external design. There are endless number of items you can add to your own decor. Take a look at what needs to be done to make you feel more "special". Your uniqueness is what gives a first impression to your guests in your life events. What is the atmosphere you are wanting to create? Know that you set the tone of your special event life. It is your self-expression and it can have an impact on your life experiences.

Designing is a way of living where your motivations, needs, and wants are positively influenced by the environment factors such as your culture, family, and location. Without your own creation of decor and design you are left with a continuation of status quo.

Chapter 5: Life's Budget – It's Your Time

Every successful event planner creates a detailed budget that balances their client's desires with their available resources. The same kind of budgeting is critical in our own lives as well.

Our lives are made up of a collection of bank accounts, with each area of our lives possessing value. You have accounts for your career, health, relationships, finances, and entertainment. A few of your accounts may have large balances, others might have respectable ones, and one or two may be overdrawn. Your career account may be solvent with daily deposits, while your health account is overdrawn through eating junk food and are not exercising regularly.

Ultimately time is your most valuable currency, so setting a budget for your main event is about allotting the limited time available to you in a way that is sufficient to meet all your needs. Where are you spending your precious time and how can you ensure all your most important accounts have balance?

When time is not budgeted properly, your accounts may be quickly depleted - especially with all of today's technological distractions. So it is important to manage yourself, and utilize your time wisely, spending it in the areas of your life that matter most to you.

Every human being receives the same daily budget of 24 hours of time allotted to them to accomplish their life's goals. You live in real time which is a world in which all time flies when you are having fun or drags when you are doing events not aligned with your purpose.

Why is it then that some people seem to manage it all with ease, while others find themselves struggling to have it all? The answer lies with how they budget their time. So the most important time of your day will be spent creating a schedule to help you do just that.

I was really good at scheduling all my work appointments. What I did not do, however, was apply those same techniques to other aspects of my life like grocery shopping, spending time with friends, or working out. Yet those are essential activities in my life that I need to invest in weekly to keep my budget balanced. Because just the same as in event planning going over-budget will cause the event to suffer in the long-term.

Life is a Special Event

It is time to remove the self-sabotage of believing you do not "have enough time," or that now is not "the right time" to manage your life's events.

The conversations, thoughts, and activities that are important to the success of your events should have a times assigned to them. This means scheduling appointments with yourself, and allowing time blocks for high-priority thoughts, conversations, and actions.

Schedule your events for when they will begin and end. Have the discipline to keep these appointments. When unplanned events arise be in communication with any of your guests or acknowledge that a new plan is to be implemented.

Plan to dedicate your time engaged in those thoughts, activities, and conversations that produce most of the results to benefit your desired events.

Take five minutes before you a make call or when working on task to decide what result you want to attain. This will help you know what success looks like before you start. In addition, it will appear to slow down time. Take five minutes after each call and activity to determine whether your desired result was achieved. If not, determine why not? How can you remedy that on your next call or activity?

Do not instantly give people your attention unless it is critical to your personal and life business to offer an immediate human response. Instead, schedule specific times to answer emails and return phone calls.

It is impossible to get everything done. Also, remember that odds are good that just 20% of your efforts produce 80% of the results.

The process of personal budget of time in planning is one of the most important things you can ever learn. However, just as with our finances, sometimes it is difficult to stay motivated to budget your time. So we need to remind ourselves that the goal of budgeting is to save time and cut down on unnecessary events that use up your hours, days, and weeks. You definitely want to budget time for fun for your mini-events and your family even if that means only going out to dinner once a month. It will still give you something to anticipate. This makes it much easier to stick to the budget.

Where are you going to invest in and get the best return for your life experiences? Each moment is yours to plan.

Auditing your life is your chance to evaluate your current distractions and revisit or uncover the real core values that drive and inspire you.

You began life with finite time and possibilities. As you go through life experiences and complete various accomplishments of school, career, marriage, and children, you may notice where you deposit most of your time. You will make adjustments regularly as a result of your audit.

No one will ever know exactly how much time you have to live. The trouble is you think you have time.

What we do know is there are factors to improve on the investments of your time. The choices you make daily will either increase or deplete your budget. What if you had an equal balance between your career, your health, and all your relationships? What a blissful moment this would be.

Your goals, your desires, and dreams are never finished – ever! Once you complete one set of goals you are ready for the next one. As soon as you manifest the next dream you will have a new adventure to undertake. Enjoy the process, the planning, and the celebrations along the way.

About the only thing you can count on today is that things will change. A production schedule can to assist you in managing changes.

Timelines are a series of events you scheduled logically. The easiest way to schedule your time might be with a calendar. You can document and completely describe all of the elements you are choosing to be produced for your special event. Put every event on the page so you will have a visual manifestation of your time and where you spend it.

There is no such thing as events without commitment. You have already made, and are living with, a host of commitments, whether or not you are aware of it. What you are committed to is revealed in what you have produced or failed to produce. Just look at the life you have created.

We are living in an increasingly demanding world and if you intend to take your place in the world then it is imperative that you learn to make and hold commitments. Setting purposed goals for your lifestyle is nothing more than an amalgam of your commitments.

Chapter 6: The Venue – It is You

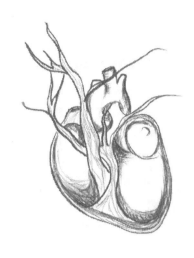

The venue for any special event is one of the most important considerations for any planner. Without it, there is no environment in which it can take place. In this case there is no need to go on an endless search for the perfect venue: you are it. ; The venue is your own physical body, your masterful mind, your expansive spirit. Your venue is alive.

You are the perfect venue to host all the moments that make up your special event life. And as you take actions consistent with your planned events you will learn through practice. And with proper preparation and planning you can improve or even upgrade your venue.

How are you going to enhance your environment for yourself that influences an extravagant setting for a life special event? You are already the most magnificent venue.

Now is the perfect time to distinguish what you need to do in order to take care of your temple for this is your destination where you will produce all your future events.

Your venue needs be attended to every day. Without proper care, you may find yourself discovering the hard way what happens when the venue is not regularly maintained.

I know firsthand what that experience is like. When an ambulance took me to hospital and I found myself with a new event team which were the doctors looking after me.

This event was as an instant warning that my health balance was depleted. Originally they thought I had a heart attack; what it turned out to be was my nervous system had frozen the nerves in my face. There would be no smile for me for the next four months of my life. I had no experience in managing such an event. It was time to call in the pros to contribute to me.

Venues may have more than one caretaker so ask for advice from mentors or experts for education on nourishing your body, healing your mind, and nurturing your soul.

People become the resources for your life. Be specific as you can to attract the suitable resources to enhance your venue for peak performance.

For example, my fitness trainer works with me to balance and strengthen my body. My naturopath applies natural therapies, and natural healing practices to monitor the internal operations of my body's systems. My specialists monitor my progress regularly. This is my event team.

For professional event managers a great deal of effort goes into creating an inviting atmosphere at the venue. Take time to outline a site inspection of your venue. This is your physical body just as it is today. Next develop a new plan for how you will manage your maintenance.

Areas I improved for me included sleep, water intake, weight, the color of my hair, my holidays, and my personal favourite, my nails (having well-manicured hands and feet makes me happy). Our venues have many different features to keep up both internally and externally.

Consider possible upgrades for your venue in the near future. You can transform your venue with simple enhancements at any given moment and affect the mood and tone for your life events.

It is also important to take into consideration the operations of your venue including financial, relationships, and your lifestyle.

It is true your venue is operating seven days a week, 24 hours nonstop.

You may want to space out the events in your life to give yourself time to rejuvenate from your work commitments. Most of us are well-trained to work, we are not as well-trained to make sure that we create pleasurable moments for ourselves every day. Set aside small indulgences for you treating yourself as the best guest. You are the VIP after all in this party.

Most venues come with catering agreements. But what about your venue? Do you plan for all your meals? Are you squeezing them in without thought? Or worse, do not forget to eat and find yourself at a cash buffet without a meal plan.

If you are not planning you may see that you are at the effect of what is offered? Here is when you find yourself having fast food delivered to your venue. Do you really want fast food to be served at this exquisite venue? The choice is always yours. Keep in mind that if you choose fast food, the integrity of your venue will suffer. Do not put your venue at risk – this is the only one you have.

Imagine a venue left for months without care and then suddenly guests show up for an event. Are you prepared to deal with the demand? How much dust and clutter do you need to clear out to allow it to function at full capacity?

Some venues require contracts that set forth clearly the terms so that each party you engage with knows the rights and responsibilities associated with it. Be clear on what you want, and how you and your partners will work together to make your events happen.

You may also need permits for your venue as required. These may include things like a passport, license, or insurance, or even medications and treatments that ensure the security and safety of your venue. Always make sure critical permits are up to date and easily accessible to you.

When people come into contact with your venue enjoy being the host. Invite people to your venue who will respect it with love, acceptance, and kindness. Your inspiration will see others taking on purpose in their own venues.

Special events are spectacular. As the host venue where all your events take place take time and appreciate all the beauty in you.

Chapter 7: Life's Delicious Menu

Every good planner works with their catering team to find the perfect menu. Yet in our own lives, many of us give little care and attention to this critical part of successful event planning.

Are you giving enough thought to the type of food you are serving yourself and are you designing meal plans with foods that fuel you? You are the number one guest in your venue and your menu should reflect your needs.

Event professionals use the expert knowledge of chefs to design menus customized to the audience. You can utilize that same expertise with the abundance of education available to you in the form of books, television, and websites.

For special events, entire departments are dedicated to planning meals for guests with regard to the exact number of meals, budget, and guarantee on the actual number of meals consumed. They are doing this work for complete strangers, don't your special guest deserve as much attention?

Event managers spend countless hours reviewing menu costs, seasonal considerations, dietary restrictions, and presentation. Menus are finalized a minimum of 72 hours in advance to allow time for shopping, selecting the best ingredients, and prepping. You can apply the same principles to your own meal planning.

Daily menu planning takes practice. Start out by tracking your meals for a week to learn about your meal habits.

Then create a weekly plan and that takes into scheduling issues and your finances. Some days you may eat on the go, and other days you may take the time to prepare, cook, and serve your own chosen meals.

Take note of which foods boost your energy. The idea here is to consider what you will enjoy the most based on the type of lifestyle you choose.

Creating a menu also means providing options to ensure that guests' various needs are met; no one wants to eat the same meal day after day. And whether it is served plated or as a buffet, meals should be colourful, fragrant, and most important, appetizing. The presentation of food should make you want to eat it.

By approaching your meal prep as though it was fuelling a special event you will start to notice the benefits. You might eat out less. You will always have the groceries you need. But you will also waste less and save money.

By organizing, you will also have in place contingency plans for those busy days. There is no more pointless staring at the fridge and cupboards wondering, "What the heck am I going to make?"

Beverages are also a part of every successful catering plan. Healthy people meet their fluid needs by drinking when thirsty and drinking fluids with meals.

To function properly, the body requires between one and two liters of water per day to avoid dehydration. Water regulates body temperature and raises the metabolism. You may find getting enough water over the course of the day is a challenge.

People at special events may be distracted by the experience s and forget to drink. If this is what you experience it may be useful to use a water tracking app or even have a reminder put into your schedule. Have water for your venue every day.

It is important to evaluate and review your plan weekly and to adjust according to your needs.

Life is a Special Event

Choose an environment that supports your life objectives for your scheduled meals.

Once your human needs of delicious meals is managed you can expand your menu planning with the choices you make in life.

Chapter 8: Your Life Entertainment

No special event is complete without entertainment, in whatever form. It inspires, provokes, and brings pleasure to its guests. Arranging entertainment for the special event that is your life means prioritizing your emotional and spiritual well-being, so choose your entertainment with great care. If you are not accustomed to making yourself a priority this is now the time to look at what makes you the happiest. And then go out and do it regardless of what anyone else thinks or says about your actions.

Remember that sometimes the best entertainment in life is free – and right in front of you. It does not cost you anything to go for a walk in the park, to read a book from the library, or to enjoy the beauty of your pets playing.

Maybe it involves your favourite cup of coffee or tea, a beautiful sunrise in the morning, a cozy sweater, your favourite yoga pants, or a delicious meal in your slow cooker. It may be as simple as hanging up a quote that inspires you or a picture that makes you feel peaceful and calm. You may also feel renewed by trying something new.

Most people today are so busy with life work they make no time for family, friends, or themselves. I have learned that even if my schedule is full I have to take fifteen minutes to be with my friend for a coffee moment. You can intentionally create entertainment to fulfill your life with happiness. Special moments become memories spent now.

Take this opportunity to look at your life and see what inspires you; what moves you with joy, happiness, or evokes a sense of adventure in you? This type of entertainment can light up your life for a moment. Entertainment gives your life its charm and energy. Without entertainment, life is dull and dreary.

Many of us listen to musical vibrations and lyrics that reflect your desires. Music embeds memories in our minds that inspire emotions in an act of spontaneous entertainment. As part of your planning each quarter I invite you to choose a piece of music that connects you to your theme. You may notice the activities around you align with that selection of music.

Make sure you invite your special guests to your live performances - doing so can enhance your enjoyment of entertainment greatly.

Chapter 9: A Live Production

The moment an event goes "live" a variety of production elements have to come together to make it all work. Production is the execution of all these events in real time. There is production happening internally in your body as a natural function and there are external factors of production.

As an event manager you have to be mindful when selecting the resources to support your event. Each device has to be appropriately integrated into the event.

Here is the good news. The system and equipment you need are already installed in your venue. You have all the power, sound, lighting, projection, and even special effects pre-installed in you.

Audio

In your venue there is a built-in DJ operating 24 hours a day. In fact as you read these words that DJ is adding a running commentary to every word and every thought you have.

Notice how your mind is constantly assessing your thoughts and actions.

In the special events world as planners we constantly adjusting audio according to the environment.

You are the master DJ of your own thoughts. Stop for a moment and listen. Is the sound of your thoughts very loud? Are you listening to the voices in your head versus being present in your live event happening in real world? You can adjust your sound in an instant.

Your internal DJ is your judgment of self and is the first to point out your faults in great detail. When something goes wrong, it runs a pre-recorded message of "I told you so!" and "Why would you do that?"

Your DJ does not want you to change your favourite song. It plays it over and over again. It is evaluating your every move. When you engage with your DJ and make specific song requests you can change the beat for your event. When you are fully conscious of your music it compliments your theme and is an inspiration.

When you choose your song recognize the power of language or lyrics. What are the lyrics of your song currently playing? When you repeat phrases enough they can become your reality whether or not it actually is the case.

Listen to yourself for a day and try to assess whether what you say to others reflects your actual experiences. You can reference your blueprint for the experience you want your life to have.

Once you understand how language shapes your life, you will have one of the finest audio systems available to your special event.

Power

Every function needs a reliable power source. It ensures the energy and vitality of the event so it is important to keep your personal power supply super-charged. Too many of us are walking around today only half-charged or our batteries are dwindling. Your energy is the fuel needed to fulfill your dreams.

Event managers bring in back up power for red carpet events because there are no retakes. This ensures that despite any challenges there will be power which ensures continuity and seamless production. You have to have a back-up power supply for yourself also.

How you do this is correlated to how you experience life. If you have increased confidence, a strong foundation of balance with optimum care for yourself, and efficiency, this gives you a high charge with natural power.

What is the energy experience you want generated in your special event?

To assess where your power source is at is simple. Ask yourself am I fully energized in all that I do? Or am I feeling tired, anxious, stressed, exhausted, and overwhelmed? Is my energy fully charged or is depleted or being diverted to another event?

This is the power of stress that can reduce the quality of your special event and even shorten it. Living a life for which you have no passion wastes precious personal power that could be spent creating the special event you really want to attend.

In order to have a full power within yourself you have to return to your most basic program so you can follow the right path starting from scratch.

The blueprint you created helps you to build your program and delete everything that no longer suits you and what no longer serves your life purpose. Your power will increase as you remove all the elements that do not charge you.

If you are honest towards your feelings and if you recognize your own truth nothing will disturb your power and balance.

Focus your power on the elements you choose and give it your best performance. Charge your life events with vitality and purpose.

Video

Visualize your events in your mind as if they are a live show. Be in your thoughts as if that show is happening now. If you have never produced a live show before then imagine your event as a movie. Be as specific as you like.

You are the projector – your thoughts are the running show or movie. Is your production focusing on what you want in your event? If it is not focused you may find the video is being blurred or corroded by other distractions in life.

Begin to notice where your thoughts are directed. Are they set-up as rear projection and looking at your past events? Or are they focused forward on your future events you created?

Imagine that your authentic self is an image projected on a wall. In the beginning, the image is crisp and focused.

The projection of your life may get out of hand when events in the world bump into your projector. Upsets, challenges, and difficulties jolt and shake it so that the image blurs.

Your own response to these events contribute to the shimmying and shaking. Now when you look up at the wall you see only a hodgepodge of fuzzy lines and motley colours. Your authentic self has fallen completely out of focus because along the way you forgot to stop and refocus.

Find out what has caused the distortions in your life. For example, you thought your marriage would last a lifetime and it ended in divorce. You trusted everyone and were taken advantage of by a friend. Life sends us many jolts but we have to learn how to readjust our settings to remain crisp and clear.

Production Schedule

The production schedule is what ties together all of the elements that will be produced for your event. It details all of the tasks with specific start and stop times from beginning to the end of the designated time you have created for your event. In this book we chose a 90 day period.

Every day there are hundreds of tasks to manage on the elements we have focused in your venue, catering, decor, entertainment, production and invitations.

Communicate your plans in writing clearly and with the timelines you intend to accomplish your events. Then you can constantly reference this to improve on ways to best allocate your time in the most efficient manner.

A good creative producer remains calm, focused and patient at all times.

Enjoy the multi-sensory experience of your event production. Come through loud and clear with your talents. Live production is what differentiates events and is designed to support and enhance your events.

Chapter 10: Scripting the Plan

You organize and celebrate your life events. For most people, no matter how good your intentions may be, the world will come at you faster than you can keep up.

Many of us seem to have it in our nature to consistently entangle ourselves in more than we have the ability to handle.

You are the artist of your life events. You are managing your elements efficiently, effectively, and with choice and thus you will have fun making choices aligned with your purpose. Choose vibrant colours, tones, and patterns that inspire you.

When you book yourself with back-to-back events all day, go to after hour events, generate more new ideas and commitments we need to deal with, and get embroiled in engagements and projects that have the potential to spin our creative intelligence into cosmic orbits.

This is precisely what makes it essential to capture and create detailed the events in your life every day. Your thoughts are your production script and they ride you taking you anywhere you want. The key here is to master you by having clarity and clear plans. Reviewing, reevaluating, and reprocessing time is required to keep you in balance.

Are you living your life according to a script? You plan your own plan for there is no one to plan it for you. Are you doing what you are doing, where you choose to do it, and with whom? When you go off your timeline, the planner distinguishes what needs to get you back on track.

What is the script is running your life? A script gives a detailed description of how and when everything happens. It is what gives your event meaning.

We would agree that the script affects the choices made for the entire production; location, scenery, casting, dialogue. You know how your life as a special event turns out. It is alive and active guiding you in what to do and say.

Gather all your plans and decide what requires you to take action. Process any notes about anything you agreed to do and do it. Review your previous week's events and see if there is anything you missed. Review your upcoming calendar, and make a note to prepare for any assignments for your plan to be completed.

Review your actions lists daily and weekly. Review your project list and consider what needs to be put into place to keep the events rolling and on target.

Finally review your life plan and re-read your original blueprint. Add important items to your agenda. A good plan executed with detail is better than a perfect plan.

This is the secret to staying on top of your priorities to schedule regular times to review and reflect. Remember that a script governs what you say and do; it also imposes expectancies or roles on other people.

Project yourself into each and every script. Write as much detail as possible as you can for your life script. Do not filter yourself. Do not try to please anyone or even to think about whether your ideas are appropriate. Let yourself dream.

Give this "dream script" enough of your time and energy and creativity for it to have some real meaning. Explore the experience you want and write it out.

Chapter II: Life's Invitations

Obviously no event is complete without guests, so it is time now to send out invitations. Drafting a guest list gives you the opportunity to examine your everyday plans in life and then use this newfound awareness to include only the best guests at your event.

Private invitations are those you give to yourself. Another form of invite is for cherished events where you directly engage with people whose relationships shape your life.

You may have noticed that people are often changing plans frequently, giving reasons and excuses as to why they cannot attend an event, or even worse, not RSVPing at all. In events and in life this can seriously affect your plans.

Both personally and professionally, I know what it feels like to be expecting someone, to put all the effort into preparations for them, only to not have them show up. It leaves us with question and disappointment.

Your life events matter. Make sure you show up to the events you created. Way too often we tend to go off our own plans to attend other people's events. You have taken the time to organize and plan this important event so let's have you have it happen.

VIP Invitations

Your first invites should be exclusively for you and you alone. This invitation is the life events you created in your blueprint for becoming an exceptional human being. Accepting the invitation means being honest with yourself, acknowledging that an area of life that is not as you desire it to be. You have created a new future, and this is how you will get to this future event.

As an example, invite yourself to an event that focusses on your sleep, your vitamin plan, your water intake, or daily meal planning. Once you accept the invitation to focus on this particular area of your life, you will choose to attend all these events. When you do this you are fulfilling on your desires.

Accepting the invite and treating it as you would any RSVP by writing it down or putting it into existence in your calendar. Add some flare to how your write it by adding descriptive details as if the event has already happened. When you create an invitation and put it into your calendar you use this to manage all your life events, it becomes more real.

From my research I discovered my current habits for breakfast, coffee, and starting my work day. These routine events of my life were sporadic, and often resulted in many unplanned events. This is when I realized that I was not planning any events for me in my calendar. All my scheduled events were work events.

I created a VIP invitation for planning my morning events. I now have ten-step plan, before I start my workday that is focused on taking care of me. It includes my morning gratitude, vitamins, breakfast, coffee, water, exercising, meditating, scheduling, and reviewing my blueprint. This is when I accomplished an entirely new lifestyle and upgraded my health balance.

VIP Invitations are for managing personal events for yourself and your life. These are among the most important ones you will ever send and accept.

General Admission Invitations

Now we can move on to general admission invitations where you engage with people in your life. Every day you have the opportunity to invite others join you in your life events. A very select few will join you for the duration of your life's most special event.

So who are the guests for your events? Not a day goes by without a moment worth celebrating. But not everyone in our life needs to be at every event so think carefully about your invitations.

The right guests can make or break an event. Powerful people create powerful alliances with others; they have resources and allow people to contribute to them. They network through life's events.

The right people arrive to assist you in every aspect of your special event life. People support you in your career, your home, your finances, your health, your transportation, and your choice in a life partner.

The list of guests is endless. People at special events are happy and fulfilled. Be ready and willing to receive your guests at any time.

As event professionals, in the invitation process, we create detailed profiles of our special guests. We have checklists of schedules and define each event with description. Invitations provide details on what attire to wear for the events, directions, and how to communicate involvement with RSVP.

A well thought out invitation takes time to design, and requires timelines in advance to allow others to schedule you into their scheduled lives.

When inviting people it is important that you choose your words wisely to reflect the type of event you are inviting people to attend and how they can participate. Each component of your invite is designed to generate a specific response. When you carefully craft these components into your communication, the most important response is to build anticipation by acceptance and attendance. This invites are any work or personal events where you intend to meet with other people.

By being as detailed as the pros, you can expect the best guests to RSVP with a yes and they will show up. Each yes, is directly impacting your overall strategic plan.

When you show your guests respect through your invitations, you will ensure your event's success. People will have sufficient time to put an invitation into their calendars. If guests in your life receive invitations just a couple of days or hours before an event, it could result in a very poor turnout.

Accepting Invitations

You will receive many invitations from people in your life. These invites show up daily in the form of calls, text messages, written requests, or even in our conversations. It is important to train yourself on how to best choose where to spend your time and RSVP accordingly.

You may find yourself accepting many life invitations too easily. Before you accept an invitation to an event, think about the amount of time that you have to invest in order to attend. Just take a moment to ask yourself does this event align with the timing of your own plans. Once you have considered all the possible impacts of your participation you can respond to invites with ease. Adjust plans to accommodate those events you will be attending. Put it into your calendar of events, and be sure to add what your intentions are in going to this event.

There are invites you will choose to decline. Saying "no" to an invitation is just as powerful as saying "yes," as both responses will affect your own schedules and blueprints. It takes practice and discipline to manage invites to ensure they only have positive impacts on your quality of life.

Life's Invitations

Everything you experience in life is the result of an invitation. Either you have created a VIP invitation or you are being invited by others. Invitation etiquette applies to both guests and hosts. In your life it is really all about how to get along with other people by treating them the way you would like to be treated. It is ideal to respond in a timely manner whether or not you can accept an invitation. If you receive an e-mail or call ideally respond within 48 hours.

If you do not know whether or not you can attend an event, you should at least call your invitee and give him or her a heads up. There is nothing worse than wondering if an invitation has been received and if so, why the person is taking so long to respond.

An event requires a lot of time and energy, not to mention expense. Yet many say they have to call invited guests to check on their response even when the invitations have been given well in advance.

And for those invitations you give to yourself, be honest in keeping your RSVP as planned, for these are the events that you created for you in your plan.

Scheduling tools are available to help you keep track of all these grand events in your life event. Keep the existence of your invitations for every area of your life including your career, your health, and relationships in a calendar.

Without scheduling, you may find your perceived reality of where you spend time is an illusion. Even a weekly trip to the grocery store can take an hour in your day. Life's simple events are the ones you want to manage the most.

Everyone you meet in your life is a guest. You may want to keep an up-to-date list of your guests. You never know when you want to invite them to future celebrations.

Even though you have treated them to an event, remember that guests often invest a lot of time in travelling to meet you. Your special guests will appreciate you acknowledging the effort they made to attend and that you sincerely appreciated them being at your event.

Chapter 12: Capture Life

Special events can feel like they pass by in a second, so capturing those moments is always important. Our lives are made up of millions little moments and it is important to capture the ones that matter.

Life is full of milestone moments worth celebrating. You can capture your events with amazing photos or by writing your life stories. Special events are a series of experiences.

Today we are all learning from each other whether it be from the photos you share or in your beautiful life experiences.

By simply documenting the events around you, you find ways to show the results of your efforts. Photography is one method of recording history and sharing emotional truth. A photograph documents reality caught in an instant by using light to capture a moment in time. Striking the balance between being the photographer who documents the event and being truly present and engaged with your event can be a challenge.

Practice being your authentic self. Be you. In today's world of "selfies," you can have lots of fun capturing you.

Social media has given you the opportunity to follow and share your event moments every day. The old cliché, pictures are worth a thousand words, rings true.

Once your life's special events are complete, the photos and stories can serve as a reminder and as an opportunity to review and evaluate, and to create inspiration for forthcoming events in your life.

When you look at your events you have accomplished go on a rampage of appreciation for all that you have, all that you are, and all that you have observed in the experiences.

Use your photos and notes as reference to evaluate the success of events, and to determine where improvements can be made in future.

Have fun reviewing those life moments you captured. After all you are the artist who created that moment.

Conclusion

Give yourself a round of applause. The fact that you are at the end of this book says a lot about who you are. You have a purposeful life plan, focused on the life events that matter most to you. Celebrate all that you are, you are special, and your life matters.

You put your heart and soul into planning your best self. Be generous as you master these skills in becoming your own event manager.

This is the red carpet of living an extraordinary life. This carpet is endless, limitless, and just for you and your special guests. As you walk this red carpet, here are a few things I want you to remember.

Breathe. The greatest favour you can offer yourself on the red carpet is to breathe deeply. Have access to a mirror before you walk the red carpet and look in the mirror regularly. Be authentic and loving with yourself. Seize your moment. Bring your best guests with you.

Have your DJ repeat to yourself these things to yourself daily: I am special. I am unique. I am worthy of my red carpet life.

Life is a Special Event

While it is okay to take a little bit of direction from other producers you meet, do not feel you have to do whatever they tell you to do. This is your life and appreciate the choices you make every day.

Do not take your life too seriously. Life is really simple so have a sense of humour and roll with the punches. Be proud, be joyous, be purposeful.

Life is a Special Event. Celebrate you every day.

About The Author

Carol Moxam, is the chief lifestyle and leadership coach at her own practice. She has been involved in the events industry for more than twenty years, and has worked a communications and life balance coach for over a decade. Prior to becoming a coach, she served in a variety of roles educating, mentoring, and teaching the next generation of leaders in the events industry, primarily in event management and entrepreneurship.

Carol has two teenage sons and resides in Oakville, Canada. She is working on her passion project, "Your Life is a Special Event," which is focused on telling the stories of global event professionals and leaders who are making a difference in their communities while living fulfilled, balanced, and purposeful lives.

Carol's trains and motivates hundreds of individuals to live a "life as a special event." She travels often and always balances her work with plenty of time for fun.

You can find out more about Carol and her work at her blog, Life is a Special Event, www.carolmoxam.com/blog and on Facebook Page www.facebook.com/LifeisaSpecialEvent

Manufactured by Amazon.ca
Bolton, ON